AUTHOR'S PREFACE

Attitudes toward the more unusual creatures are generally more favorable today than they have been in the past. Conservationists have shown us the very real fear and realization that many exotic animals are on a frighteningly fast decline in population, due largely to man's destruction, or, at the very least, alteration, of the environment "for economic gain." We are, apparently and unfortunately, witnessing the fastest demise of biological diversity in the history of life itself! The Green Iguana is one of those animals that is threatened.

I have written this small book especially for those people who have a soft spot for Green Iguanas. Those of you who have an uncontrollable urge to own one, or (more preferably) a pair, will find all you need to know to keep them in the best of health (and perhaps breed them) right here in this handy little guide. Additionally, this book will hopefully be of some interest to the general naturalist who may like to learn a bit more about the Green Iguana's life history and so forth.

As a person who has been fanatical about reptiles for most of his life and has worked with them both professionally and as a hobby, I have always had a special affection for *Iguana iguana*. I hope this little book will lead many iguanaphiles into the years of interest and pleasure that they can provide.

John Coborn
Nanango, Queensland

ISABELLE FRANCAIS

The Green Iguana, *Iguana iguana*, is perhaps the most popular reptile pet in the world. They can be purchased almost any place that sells reptiles and amphibians.

THE GREEN IGUANA

RANGE AND HABITAT

The Green Iguana occurs in suitable habitats from southern Mexico to central South America, including some Caribbean Islands. It has, however, become very scarce or even absent from many of its former haunts, probably due to overcollection and loss of habitat. There are successfully introduced populations in the areas of Miami and Fort Lauderdale in Florida.

The Green Iguana occurs in a variety of habitats, most predominantly from open woodland to rainforest. It usually haunts areas where good cover is available, such as among trees or thick vegetation, or on boulder-strewn river banks. It is an adept climber and spends varying amounts of time basking among tree branches or foraging on the ground. One of its favorite resting places is a bough overhanging the water into which it will dive and take refuge if disturbed.

TIDBITS STUDIO

Green Iguanas are not particularly difficult to maintain in captivity and newborn specimens are very inexpensive.

DESCRIPTION

With a maximum length of 6.5 ft/2 m (of which two-thirds is taken up by the laterally flattened, whiplike tail), the Green Iguana is a large, robust, and spectacular lizard. The body is upright oval in section while the head is relatively large and the snout is rounded. Each of the well-developed limbs end with five digits tipped with sharp claws. There is a conspicuous, comb-edged, erectable dewlap under the chin and throat. A particular characteristic of this species is the group of large scales situated just below the ear, one of which may be over 0.5 in/1 cm in diameter in adult specimens. There is a crest of comb-like spines extending from the neck into the first third of the tail. The longest spines, on the nape, may be up to 0.6 in/1.5 cm high. The body is covered with relatively small, granular scales. There is a number of larger, raised, cone-shaped scales on the neck, and the head is covered with large, plate-like scales.

The animal is predominantly green to grayish in color, growing darker with age. Some very old specimens appear almost black. There are dark bands across the shoulders and tail and there may be a bluish tinge around the upper forelimbs. The large and small scales below the prominent external eardrum are whitish with a tinge of green. The underside is lighter green to off-

Opposite: One of the most appealing aspects of the Green Iguana is that small specimens are safe with children.

It is a good idea to regularly handle a Green Iguana while it's still small so it will be tame when it grows large. Photo by Isabelle Francais.

BEHAVIOR

An extremely adept climber, the Green Iguana uses its strong claws to scale the trunks and limbs of trees. It prefers trees with a large, green canopy and it rests or basks on limbs (preferably overhanging water) into which it will dive and make its escape if threatened. Should there be no direct access to water, a green iguana will drop from a tree to the ground, landing on all fours, the limbs acting as shock-absorbers much like those of a cat. With a remarkable turn of speed it then rushes off into nearby cover.

Being an excellent swimmer, the Green Iguana is very much at home in the water and sometimes even browses on aquatic vegetation. When under threat from a predator, it may take to the water, diving deeply and using its long, flattened, undulating tail to propel it speedily in the direction of cover. The limbs are not used for swimming propulsion but may be used for stabilization and piloting. The Green Iguana hides among aquatic vegetation or among the submersed roots of waterside trees and shrubs, only bringing its head and nostrils above the water surface until it is assured that it can safely emerge.

The long tail is used as a balancing aid during the reptile's climbing activities. Although not exactly prehensile, the tail can be used as a steadying or thrusting aid to locomotion. It is also used as a weapon of defense, being lashed in a

white. Some specimens show splashes of reddish brown to yellow on various parts of the body.

The sexes are very similar but the dewlap and crests of the male are generally larger than those of the female. The male's head is also more robust, the coloration and pattern more vivid, and there is a row of well-developed glandular pores under the hind-thighs (these are only vestigial in the females). Juvenile Green Iguanas have only a poorly developed crest and dewlap and are almost wholly bright grass-green in color.

whiplike fashion and aimed at a potential adversary. Anyone who has had a lash across the face from a Green Iguana's tail will vouch for its efficiency in this function! However, if cornered or seized, the Green Iguana uses not only its tail in defense but also its pointed claws, which are capable of ripping into the human skin. The Green Iguana's sharp, serrated teeth should also be treated with respect. Thankfully, such brusque defensive behavior is soon lost by captive specimens, who can usually be handled with reasonable safety once they are accustomed to you (although you should always be aware that they can still unintentionally scratch you with their claws).

Belly of a young Green Iguana. Photo by W. P. Mara.

Like many lizards, a Green Iguana can shed most or part of its tail by a process known as autotomy. It does not, however, do this as readily as some other lizards do. Many can do it voluntarily by muscle contraction. The tail breaks at one of several predetermined planes of weakness across the tail-vertebrae rather than between two vertebrae, as was once thought. In many lizard species, autotomy is an aid to defense—the lizard makes its escape while the predator is dealing with the wriggling, cast-off tail. In the case of the Green Iguana, however, the tail is cast only as a last resort.

PREDATION

Green Iguanas are preyed upon by a variety of animals in the wild. Large constricting snakes like the boas and the anacondas will prey upon adult Green Iguanas while the juveniles are preyed upon by smaller snake species. Caimans, large freshwater turtles, and even large freshwater fish all take their toll. Birds of prey and carnivorous mammals, including otters, bears, jaguars and other wild cats, find Green Iguanas much to their liking. Amerindian tribes have also included Green Iguanas on their menus for generations. All of these predators had little impact on populations of Green Iguanas because they are a natural part of their ecology.

When European man arrived on the South American continent, however, this spelled disaster for both Green Iguanas and many other animal species as well. In some areas, human populations have increased a thousandfold, with resulting losses of habitats. Living and breeding sites for Green Iguanas have been replaced by housing developments, mines, factories, wharves, agricultural areas, ball parks, and so on. The Amerindians still continue to eat the Green Iguanas that are left and, to make matters even worse, the new Americans have added it to their menu, as have their dogs, cats, and pigs. And all the time, collectors are still capturing them to sell as pets!

CONSERVATION

The efforts of conservationists in recent years have persuaded the governments of many countries to see the importance of preserving their varieties of wildlife, and now Green Iguanas are listed in the appendices of the Convention on International Trade in Endangered Species of Wild Flora and Fauna (CITES) which means that international trade of the species is only allowed under special license. Beyond that, there are strict regulations with regard to the capture, restraint, husbandry, and transport of all specimens. All of this, of course, is a big reason why captive breeding of our reptiles is of utmost importance. If species become even more endangered (as they inevitably will), then the breeding of captive stock will be the only way to produce further specimens for the enthusiasts.

While many governments are paying lip service to these conservation procedures (particularly when dealing with other countries), many more seem lackadaisical in enforcing the laws within their own countries. Another problem exists when a neighboring country is indifferent to illegal imports from a country that might well be endeavoring to apply its wildlife protection laws. What is required to save animals like Green Iguanas is that a number of habitats be declared as national parks and thus strictly protected from any form of exploitation. Furthermore, if Green Iguana flesh is to be continually used as a commodity, then iguana farms should be set up in the reptiles' natural habitats, where they can be protected and bred commercially in large numbers. A few such farms are apparently already operating in the hopes of supplying the large pet markets of Europe and North America.

W. P. MARA

The claws of a large Green Iguana can cause serious cuts and bruises, so be careful when lifting any large specimens.

CLASSIFICATION

Green Iguanas are classified in the suborder Sauria. Within the Sauria there are 19 families of lizards with over 3000 species overall. The Green Iguana and all of its relatives are placed together in the family Iguanidae. Each group of iguanids is placed in a lesser group called a genus. The Green Iguana, *Iguana iguana*, shares its genus with only one other species, the rare Caribbean Iguana, *Iguana delicatissima*.

ISABELLE FRANCAIS

Although many Green Iguanas are captive-bred every year, many more are taken from the wild. When purchasing your pet, remember that the captive-bred specimens are generally more desirable.

Closeup of the Green Iguana head. Notice the enlarged scale below and just behind the ear. This is a trademark of the species.

HOUSING GREEN IGUANAS

There are really no hard and fast rules with regard to housing Green Iguanas but there are a few things that you should take into account. A cage in which Green Iguanas or other reptiles are kept is usually called a terrarium or vivarium (I will use the former in this book). The terrarium should be of sufficient size and must be supplied with the necessary life-support systems (heating, lighting, humidity, ventilation, etc.). Additionally, it should be easy to clean and service, must be escape-proof, and have an attractive appearance if you wish to use it as a display item.

The shape of the terrarium is unimportant as long as the parameters are large enough to give your captive a fair amount of room in which to thrive. You could buy a ready-made terrarium, complete with all its life-support systems already intact, but many enthusiasts still prefer to make their own. Such enclosures may be constructed from various materials, and many keepers get immense pleasure out of such creative work.

With silicone rubber sealant, it is possible to construct glass terrariums of many shapes and sizes. And, by using a combination of glass and acrylic (Plexiglas) materials, you can have ventilation holes drilled in the sides or back (it is fairly easy to drill holes in acrylic sheeting). The lid for a glass terrarium should preferably be made of plywood or plastic and should form a cavity in which the heating and lighting apparatus can be concealed from

Opposite: Never lift a large Green Iguana in this manner. Even if you grasp it at the base of the tail there is still the chance the tail may break off. Photo by Isabelle Francais.

view from the outside. It is best to cover the apparatus with wire mesh so that the inmates cannot gain access to it and burn themselves. The minimum size of the tank for a pair of juveniles (up to one year old) should be about 3 cubic feet/0.25 cubic meters.

You can use timber to construct a terrarium but the wood must have a few coats of varnish or non-toxic paint or it will quickly deteriorate in damp situations. A simple terrarium for juvenile Green Iguanas consisting of a plywood box with a framed glass front is easy to make. Using 0.5 in/ 10 mm plywood, the top, bottom, and ends are simply glued and nailed together. A terrarium with dimensions 36 in x 18 in x 18 in/91 cm x 45 cm x 45 cm is adequate for a pair of young Green Iguanas.

A glass viewing panel can be slid into grooves on the top and bottom or in the sides. You may also wish to mount the glass in a wooden frame, which can be attached to the front of the cage with hinges. Groups of ventilation holes should be drilled through the ends of the cage about one-third the distance up from the base to the top. Further holes should be drilled in the top to allow for convection. A sliding metal, plastic, or wooden tray can be fitted in the base of the box to hold the substrate and simplify cleaning operations.

A pair of adult Green Iguanas will, of course, require a much larger cage. Though you can make such a cage from scratch, I have seen many fine terrariums produced by transforming old wardrobes or chests of drawers from which the insides and doors have been removed. You may be able to get some old aluminum or timber framed windows from a demolition yard and incorporate these into the setup. The minimum dimensions should be 6 ft x 6 ft x 3 ft/180 cm x 180 cm x 90 cm.

THE PERMANENT TERRARIUM

A really substantial terrarium for Green Iguanas could be built with concrete blocks or bricks and could include a permanent, drainable, concrete pool and an artificial cliff face with ledges. Built-in to a part of the house or apartment, such a setup could be a focal point in the den, living room, hall, or conservatory. It could be made in an alcove or it could be free-standing. A visit to a zoological collection which has a reptile house will no doubt give you several further ideas.

A word of warning—before commencing any major construction, be sure you are not violating any building regulations. Also, it may be a good idea to get some engineering or plumbing advice before undertaking any work that is beyond your capabilities.

TERRARIUM FURNISHINGS AND DECORATIONS

Your Green Iguana cages will require various furnishings which are

DAVID R. MOENCH

Green Iguanas love to climb, so if you're thinking of bringing your outside, be careful. You don't want to end up chasing after them!

both functional and decorative. Although it is possible to keep Green Iguanas in almost "clinical" conditions (a sheet of absorbent paper, a water dish, and a hiding box), most enthusiasts want a terrarium that is a decorative feature in their home. However, the clinical method can still be convenient if you want to keep several breeding pairs or colonies, plus it is easy to maintain.

Floor Coverings: These are many and varied but it is perhaps best to use washed gravel which can be obtained in various grades. Pea-sized gravel is perhaps best for Green Iguanas. Do not use very fine sand as it tends to cake between a Green Iguana's scales. Whatever substrate material you use, it must be removed and washed, or replaced, at regular intervals.

Rocks: Available in a very wide range of interesting shapes and colors, rocks are not only decorative but can also be used as basking sites, hiding places, to help to keep an animal's nails trim, and to increase the area of exercise available. You may be able to get suitable rocks in your local pet store or garden center but it is much more exciting to go out on location and find your own (make sure you have permission to take rocks away from private land). Always ensure rocks are placed firmly and cannot fall down and injure the reptiles. If you are using large piles of rocks, it is best to cement them together to prevent accidents.

Logs and Branches: Strong tree branches are very important for climbing lizards like Green Iguanas. It is more practical to use dead tree branches rather than to try and grow trees or shrubs in the terrarium unless the accommodation is very large. Try and select branches with interesting shapes; gnarled and twisted limbs are always attractive to look at. Driftwood collected from the seashore or from river banks is often visually stimulating as it will have been weathered by the action of sand, sun, and water. All wood should be scrubbed thoroughly then

Four Paws Terrarium Linings are fully washable and mildew resistant.

For Green Iguanas, bark nuggets make a good substrate. Bark nuggets can be purchased in bulk and are easy to work with.

PHOTO COURTESY OF FOUR PAWS.

rinsed and dried before being used. You may want to immerse the log in a solution of bleach for a day or two to give it a more weathered appearance (but rinse it thoroughly before use to remove the excess bleach). Larger logs and branches should be securely fixed in position in the terrarium, ensuring that they cannot fall and possibly injure the inmates. Screws and wire are a convenient way of fixing them.

Plants: Vibrant living plants provide a subtle esthetic touch. However, unless the terrarium is very large, it is futile to try and grow plants where large Green Iguanas are being kept. The plants will be continually uprooted, flattened, or eaten. You will therefore have to compromise with artificial plants (fortunately, some are very realistic

Four Paws Safety Screen Covers are designed to fit any size tank. The locking system ensures the pet's safety.

in appearance) or do without plants at all.

LIFE-SUPPORT SYSTEMS

Certain life-support aids are not available in the indoor terrarium so they have to be provided with artificial systems to compensate. Such systems include heating, lighting, humidity, and ventilation.

Heating: Like all reptiles, Green Iguanas are cold-blooded, or, to use a more technical term, poikilothermic. This means that they maintain their bodies at a preferred temperature by moving in and out of warm places (by basking directly in the sun or absorbing heat from sun-warmed soil, rocks, or other items).

Allowing natural sunlight to pass through terrarium glass poses problems of overheating, though this can be overcome in the summer by using insect screening or mesh instead of glass. At other times artificial means of heating have to be employed.

Remember that Green Iguanas

Using an under-tank heating pad to warm a Green Iguana is very sensible. Such pads can be purchased at many pet shops and are offered in a variety of sizes.

require a reduction in temperature at night. In the home, this can be accomplished by simply switching off the heat source and allowing the terrarium to cool to room temperature (as long as this does not drop below 65°F/18°C). You should aim to maintain daytime temperatures between 82 and 95°F/28 and 35°C, reducing this to 65 to 72°F/ 18 to 22°C at night.

There are many heating devices you can use. Ordinary household incandescent light bulbs had long been used as a sole source of heating and lighting in the home terrarium until it was discovered that

the quality of light emitted was insufficient for diurnal basking lizards. Incandescent bulbs should not be ignored, however, as they are inexpensive, emit a fair amount of heat, and will supply supplementary light. The internal dimensions of the terrarium will dictate what size bulb(s) to use. By experimenting with various wattages and a thermometer, suitable temperatures will be arrived at. The bulb can be concealed inside a flowerpot or a metal canister and controlled by a thermostat so that a constant minimum background temperature is maintained.

COURTESY OF FINN STRONG DESIGNS

The River Tank System RT30 combines a variety of elements in to a complete ecosystem. Pools of water at different levels are connected by rapids or waterfalls and fish move freely from pool to pool. Plants grow hydroponically from a hidden gravel pocket in the rear which also acts as a biological filter. Plenty of room is available for aquatic animals and small reptiles above the river area including a "lizard ledge" which can be heated to provide an optimal environment.

Various kinds of heating-lamps are available. These produce infra-red or white radiant heat and are the same type

Any captive lizard will need the accurate replication of sunlight in order to survive. Bulbs designed specifically for this purpose can be purchased at many pet shops. Photo courtesy of Energy Savers.

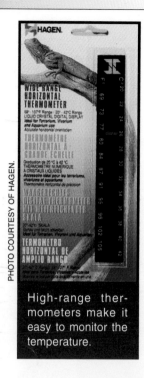

High-range ther-
mometers make it
easy to monitor the
temperature.

used in poultry brooders or piggeries.
They are great for heating basking
spots. They should be set at one end
of the cage so that there is a
temperature gradation from one end
of the cage to the other. Your Green
Iguanas will then be able to seek out
their own preferred temperatures.
Ceramic heating plates or bulbs are
also available. Sometimes referred to
as "black light" bulbs, these emit
heat but no light and are useful for
maintaining background heat at
night.

Cable heaters and pads of the type
used by horticulturists in their
propagating boxes can be used for
heating parts of the substrate. They
are good for background heat or the
provision of additional basking areas.

Aquarium heaters are useful for
maintaining warmth plus humidity
in the terrarium. Placed in the water
vessel, an aquarium heater will keep

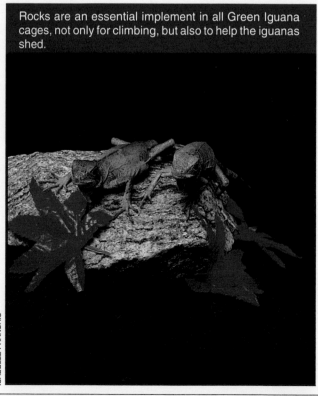

Rocks are an essential implement in all Green Iguana
cages, not only for climbing, but also to help the iguanas
shed.

the water warm and the air warm and humid. By using an aquarium aerator pump as well you will further increase humidity, help raise the air temperature, provide additional ventilation, and help keep the water fresh.

Lighting: Natural sunlight or a good substitute is very important for maintaining good health in Green Iguanas. The most important constituents of sunlight are the ultraviolet rays that help stimulate the manufacture of vitamin D3 in the skin. This vitamin is essential for controlling the actions of calcium and phosphorus in the body. Without it, various health problems will ensue. If possible, let your Green Iguanas have unfiltered natural sunlight by allowing it to pass through mesh. Natural sunlight through glass is not effective because the benefit of the ultraviolet rays is filtered out. It is impossible to place terrariums outside for most of the year in temperate areas, so compromise lighting of good quality must be provided. Special fluorescent tubes which emit a preponderance of light from the "blue" end of the spectrum will provide sufficient ultraviolet light for your pets. Be aware that too much ultraviolet light can be more damaging than too little. Research into suitable light sources for horticulture, aquariums, and terrariums is continuing, so information on suitable systems may be obtained from aquarist's suppliers or manufacturers.

PHOTO COURTESY OF ENERGY SAVERS

There are a number of products designed to provide Green Iguanas with realistic day/night cycles. The two lights shown here are good examples of such products.

Humidity: Green Iguanas require the atmosphere to be moderately humid. As most kinds of heating apparatus in the terrarium tend to create a dry atmosphere, we have to use alternate methods to include humidity. Aquarium heaters used in the water bath will help, or you can use an aerator in the water. The simplest method of maintaining humidity in a cage, of course, is to spray-mist it, but this may have to be done several times a day.

Ventilation: Adequate ventilation is very important in the close confines of the terrarium. A lack of it will lead to a buildup of stagnant air and an excess of carbon dioxide, providing favorable conditions for disease organisms to thrive and multiply, plus it will cause stress in your animals and a resulting reduced resistance to disease. Ensure, therefore, that there is a constant air exchange in the terrarium but without creating excessive cold drafts. In most cases, the provision of adequate ventilation holes in the sides and top of a terrarium is all that is required. The warmth generated by the heating apparatus will cause air convection currents, the warm air leaving through the top and fresh air replacing it through the side vents.

If a Green Iguana is kept in a glass aquarium, you will have to provide it with artificial full-spectrum lighting. Natural sunlight filtered through glass is not useful.

R.D. BARTLETT

FEEDING GREEN IGUANAS

A very important consideration to be taken into account regarding the captive diet of the Green Iguanas is that "variety is the spice of life," remembering that it is the variety that insures the balanced diet. But even with a great variety of foods, it is still considered necessary to provide additional vitamin/mineral supplements. In the wild, adult Green Iguanas feed on a variety of plant foods, including young shoots, growth. As the reptiles mature, the amount of plant food increases, replacing part of the animal diet and eventually rounding off with a plant/animal ratio of approximately four to one.

Thus, since the adult Green Iguana is about 80% herbivorous, you should offer a variety of green food and fruit. You will find that they will accept such items as fresh clover, lucerne, dandelion (leaves

Since Green Iguanas tend to bathe and drink from the same water source, it is important that you keep the water as clean as possible.

leaves, flowers and fruits. They may also occasionally take invertebrates, small vertebrates (nestling birds for example), and carrion. In other words, Green Iguanas can be regarded as omnivorous browsers that take animal food opportunistically.

It has to be assumed that the variety of foods taken by wild Green Iguanas will constitute a balanced diet. The young are largely insectivorous during their early period of growth, feeding on a variety of invertebrates but also taking a small amount of plant food as well. The invertebrate food is important in providing adequate protein during the early period of

and flowers), sow-thistle (*Sonchus* species), spinach, and lettuce (the latter in only small amounts as a treat only as it is not very nutritious), as the staple diet, supplemented with various fruits and berries (tomatoes, cucumbers, bananas, apples, pears, pineapples, peaches, apricots, strawberries, gooseberries, blackcurrents, cherries, plums, avocados, and so on). You can also try such items as grated carrots, sweet potatoes, pumpkins, boiled potatoes, zucchinis, peas, beans, cabbages, broccoli, and so on. You will find that not all Green Iguanas will eat all items listed; it may require a certain amount of experimentation before you arrive at an ideal diet for your particular specimen. Remember also that canned fruit (pears, peaches, fruit salad, etc.) can often convert a "bad feeder" into a "good feeder."

With regard to the 20% animal part of their diet, Green Iguanas will take a variety of invertebrate foods, including mealworms, grasshoppers, and crickets. Additionally, they may be given the occasional meal of minced lean beef or ox-heart. Canned cat or dog food may be given sparingly as it is likely to be too fattening. I once had a Green Iguana that was mad about half-grown mice, so as you can see, there is no harm in trying anything that you can imagine as long as it is given in moderation (and, of course, it is of no harm to them).

Your feeding strategy may be a matter of trial and error. For example, if one of your Green Iguanas is crazy about, say, bananas, it would be best to leave these out of its diet once in a while and get the animal used to trying other foods.

A multi-mineral/vitamin supplement powder should be sprinkled over the food regularly. I would recommend a daily dish of mixed vegetable food with the addition of meat and insects twice

PHOTO COURTESY OF FLUKER FARMS.

Meal worms, crickets and other natural lizard foods are now available in convenient freeze-dried form.

per week and the vitamin/mineral supplement also twice per week.

With regard to quantities of food, that is another matter of trial and error. At first, the best method is to aim for "just a little being left in the dish" after each meal; then you will know the amount that is being eaten and will be able to reduce it slightly. You should never overfeed your Green Iguanas or they will become obese and probably infertile. It is better for captive reptiles to be slightly underfed.

Some of the livefoods suitable for juvenile Green Iguanas and as a supplement to an adult's diet are as follows:

Collected Livefoods: You can probably collect a variety of invertebrate foods for your Green Iguana during the warmer parts of the year, then you can concentrate on cultivated foods in the winter.

Probably the best method of obtaining a selection of terrestrial insects is by "foliage sweeping," passing a large, fine-meshed net (a butterfly net is ideal) through the foliage of trees, shrubs, and tall grass. Using this method, you should be able to harvest ample quantities of caterpillars, grasshoppers, beetles, and moths, which are all items that your Green Iguanas should accept. The insects can be sorted and size-graded and placed in a number of jars or small plastic containers for transport home. Use only smooth-skinned caterpillars (not the hairy varieties which can sometimes have poisonous properties). Do not put too many insects into the Green Iguana cage at any one time but instead allow the lizards to consume what is available before adding more. Otherwise, you will get escapees in your house.

Quantities of moths (many species of which will be avidly devoured by juvenile Green Iguanas) can also be caught using a light-trap, or you can use a net close to an electronic "bug-zapper."

Propagated Foods: In addition to collected foods, there will be times when we must rely on cultivated livefoods for Green Iguanas. The following is a selection of the types of livefoods that are commonly propagated, available commercially, and easy to breed at home if you wish:

Mealworms: These are the larval form of a type of flour beetle and are one of the easiest food insects to propagate. However, as a food item they are low in digestible calcium so they must be used only as part of a more varied diet. In any case, they

are best sprinkled with a little vitamin/mineral powder before being offered.

A breeding colony can be set up with about 100 mealworms placed in a large plastic tray or box with a 2 in/5 cm layer of a 50/50 mixture of chicken meal and bran. Cover them with a piece of fabric or absorbent paper, on which a few slices of carrot or potato should be placed to provide moisture. The mealworms will eventually pupate, emerging a few weeks later as adult beetles. These will mate and lay eggs, starting your next generation of mealworms. For a sustainable supply of mealworms, maintain four cultures simultaneously, starting a new one and discarding the oldest one each month.

Crickets: These are a highly nutritious food item and could be the most important item to your juvenile Green Iguanas during the winter months. They are now cultured widely and are usually readily available from pet shops or by mail order. One of the most commonly cultured species is the domestic cricket, *Acheta domestica.* The

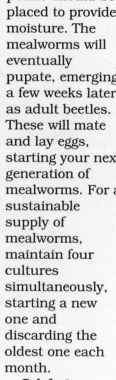

Four Paws Nature's Reptile Vita-Spray was formulated by veterinarians and herpetologists and contains vitamins that are important for reptiles' health.

By giving lots of nutrients to your iguana's food items, you will then pass those nutrients on to the iguana. That's why it's a good idea to maintain those food items on specially formulated diets. Check your local pet store for such products.

crickets can be kept in any suitably sized, escape-proof container (I have used a plastic trash can with great success, having cut out a hole in the lid and covered this with screening for ventilation purposes). Give the crickets balls of bunched up newspaper in which to hide. A small saucer, containing a piece of moistened cotton wadding or clean bath-sponge, will provide drinking water for the insects. They can be fed on cereals and greenfood (grass, lettuce, cabbage, spinach, various fruits, etc.). The adult crickets like to lay their eggs in a damp medium so provide a dish or two of moist sand or vermiculite. The dish should be removed to a separate container at regular intervals and replaced with a new one. If kept at a temperature of about 77°F/25°C, the eggs will hatch in about three weeks.

Young Green Iguanas are generally more carnivorous than the adults are. Photo by Isabelle Francais.

One of the nicest things about Green Iguanas is the fact that most of them have healthy appetites. Photo by Isabelle Francais.

The Green Iguana, *Iguana iguana*.

Tame Green Iguanas can be fed right from their keeper's shoulder. In fact, Green Iguanas are among the few reptile pets that, when tame, can be regularly fed outside their cage. Photo by Isabelle Francais.

BREEDING GREEN IGUANAS

Successful Green Iguana breeding seems to revolve around the stimulus of introducing a new male to an existing male/female pair. By keeping two adult pairs and introducing them when a breeding response is required, it is likely that

Some keepers prefer to acquire a young male/female pair of Green Iguanas and raise them up rather than buy the more expensive (and often wild-caught) adults. Photo by Isabelle Francais.

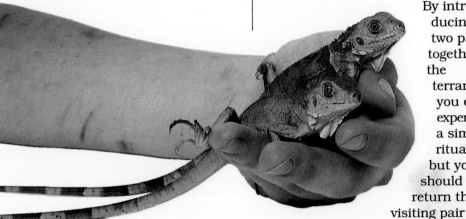

color. Should the threat fail to impress the intruder and cause him to submit (by crouching low) or retire, the intruder himself will take on a similar stance. Then, after first circling each other warily, they will eventually come to blows by banging their heads together. The process seems to be a trial of strength and courage rather than a serious fight, so individuals are rarely injured. Eventually, one of the opponents will give up and the victor is left to mate with the females.

By introducing two pairs together in the terrarium you can experience a similar ritual, but you should return the visiting pair back to their original accommodations before either male has submitted. This way you will have fooled both into thinking they have won and both will hopefully proceed to court and mate with their respective females.

Female Green Iguanas occasionally perform a similar but diluted threat ritual to that of the male, usually only in order to protect their sleeping branches but sometimes to contest for the best egglaying sites.

you will end up with both females gravid. Conversely, single pairs kept alone will often go for years without ever attempting to breed—perhaps never at all!

MALE COMBAT

Male Green Iguanas are extremely territorial in their native habitats, taking up an area of river bank with several trees and defending it vigorously against any intruding males. During such confrontations, the defending male curves his back and raises up his body by stretching his limbs to their full extent (making him appear as though his is standing on tip-toe) and presenting the side of his body toward the intruder. At the same time, his gular fold is extended and the dewlap visibly darkens in

COPULATION

Once a pair get together without interference, courtship begins. This also consists of much head-bobbing and dewlap-spreading by both sexes. Eventually the male gets on the female's back and takes her neck in

Opposite: During breeding season, adult male Green Iguanas will engage in what is called a "male combat ritual." Although this can appear quite violent to a keeper, it is a normal part of their reproductive routine.

his mouth. If the female is receptive, she will allow him to twist the rear portion of his body under hers so that their respective cloacas come into apposition. Holding her tail with one of his hind limbs he is then able to insert one of his hemipenes into her cloaca. Copulation usually takes place over a period of ten to 45 minutes.

GESTATION

It takes 50 to 100 days before the fertilized eggs are ready to be laid. To a certain extent, egg development can be hastened or slowed depending on the conditions of temperature, humidity, food supply, and so on, so that they are ready to

be laid at a favorable time. The female ceases to feed for two or three weeks before the eggs are deposited but will drink increasing amounts of water.

NESTING/EGGLAYING

Suitable nesting sites often are scarce in the wild. These take into account the aspect of the sun, the ease with which the subsoil can be excavated, and the general safety of the area. In order to avoid wholesale egg predation by humans, domestic animals, and wild animals, gravid female Green Iguanas often swim surprisingly long distances to get to uninhabited islands in rivers and estuaries. Here they will lay their eggs in burrows along sunny banks above the high water-mark. Digging out the burrows with the front limbs, the rear limbs are used to push the excavated soil back. The burrow is 3 to 6 ft/1 to 2 m long with the egglaying chamber about 2 ft/60 cm below ground level. A normal clutch consists of about 20 to 40 eggs but up to 70 have been recorded. After laying the eggs, the female fills the burrow in and then returns to her usual habitat.

If you keep your Green Iguanas in large enough enclosures

Gravid female Green Iguanas should only be handled with the greatest of care and only when absolutely necessary. Photo by Isabelle Francais.

CARLOS RAVAZZANI

Notice the tick on the dewlap of this Green Iguana. Ideally, any specimens that are suffering from any kind ailment whatsoever should not be used as breeding stock.

you can provide them with a damp sandpit about 3 ft/90 cm deep for natural egglaying. Captive female Green Iguanas are, however, often unsatisfied with the egglaying facilities provided and will end up just spreading the eggs indiscriminately over the floor of the cage. Wherever the eggs are laid,

Opposite: It is important that all Green Iguanas involved in the reproductive cycle be well fed, for those animals that are not in peak health will not do well.

they must be collected for artificial incubation because facilities in the terrarium will be far too hit-and-miss for complete success. Those which are buried in a sandpit should be carefully dug out while any laid on the cage floor (sometimes even in the water bath) should be rescued as quickly possible.

The white, leathery-shelled eggs are usually laid two at a time, with intervals between the pairs. Each egg is slightly oval, averages 1.4 x 1.0 in/ 35 x 25 mm and weighs about 10 to 12 grams.

INCUBATION

In the wild, the eggs rely on the sun-warmed earth of some tropical river bank for all the incubating. Captive-laid eggs, however, must be placed in an incubator. The soft shell is designed to absorb moisture from the substrate or incubation medium. Newly laid eggs often have dimples or collapsed areas but these flaws usually fill out as moisture is absorbed. Keep them up the same way as they were collected (mark the "top" with a non-toxic marker) and partially bury them in an incubation medium in a shallow container. For convenience, the eggs can be laid in neat rows and buried to about three-quarters of their thickness. The fourth quarter, left exposed, will allow you to inspect the eggs without disturbing them.

Many types of incubation mediums can be used (peat, sand, sawdust, paper-towels, cotton-towels etc.), but the most successful in my experience has been been granular vermiculite. This is an inert, sterile, absorbent material used for insulation and in the horticultural industry. It can be obtained in various grades and is very absorbent. It should be mixed with about its own weight of water before being placed in an incubation box. The lid of the incubation box should be provided with a few ventilation holes to allow for air circulation, but not too many because the lid also helps to conserve moisture. The box is placed in an incubator and maintained at a temperature of about 82 to 88°F/28 to 31°C.

The type of incubator used seems to be unimportant as long as the correct temperature can be provided. You can purchase a commercial incubator, but

Although all Green Iguanas, both male and female alike, should be offered plenty of food during the breeding season, some may only stare at it rather than eat it. Photo by Isabelle Francais.

since these are often rather expensive you may want to make your own instead. A perfectly satisfactory incubator can be made by using an old fish tank or a simple wooden box containing an incandescent light bulb and a thermostat. With a thermometer in the box you will be able to experiment until you are sure that the correct temperatures are being

water, but do not be in too much of a hurry to discard any eggs unless you are quite sure they have spoiled.

The period of incubation can vary from about 90 to 120 days depending on the temperature and humidity. This incubation time can be frustrating, especially for beginners. You may even be tempted to open an egg up to see if the embryo is really developing. This won't prove anything

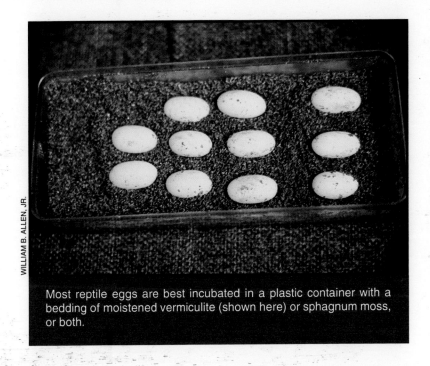

WILLIAM B. ALLEN, JR.

Most reptile eggs are best incubated in a plastic container with a bedding of moistened vermiculite (shown here) or sphagnum moss, or both.

maintained. It is best to use a red or blue bulb, or mount a regular white bulb in some sort of cover to minimize light intensity. Alternatively, a heating pad, a cable heater, or a porcelain heater may also be used. By placing a dish of water in the incubator and warming it with an aquarium heater you will be able to increase heat and supplement the humidity.

The eggs will absorb the moisture from the surrounding medium and increase in weight as the embryos develop. Infertile eggs do not absorb

except that the egg you chose was either developing or not. It may be the only viable egg in the clutch! Patience is certainly a virtue here, however, and hopefully you will be rewarded with a batch of lively little Green Iguanas.

HATCHING

When ready to hatch, baby Green Iguanas will slit open the tough, leathery egg-shell with the egg tooth, a sharp projection on the snout which is shed shortly after hatching. Once hatching has begun, the babies may seem to take a long time to free themselves from the shell (often 24 hours or more) but the temptation to "help" them is usually best avoided unless the reptile is having obvious difficulties. Occasionally the hatchling will stick tightly to the eggshell as a result of the fluids hardening by drying out too quickly. This can usually be avoided if the humidity is kept high (a gentle mist-spraying with lukewarm water may help too). If the hatchling still sticks,

heated separately on heat tapes or pads. High humidity should be maintained by having a shallow water bath in each tank and by mist-spraying with lukewarm water twice daily. It is essential that baby Green Iguanas have regular access to unfiltered sunlight or to full-spectrum lighting. Do not attempt to remove the yolk sac from the babies because once the contents have been absorbed it will soon shrivel up, leaving a tiny scar on the

W. P. MARA

Small, captive-bred Green Iguanas usually make great pets mainly because they haven't been exposed to the rigors of life in the wild.

you may have to resort to gently dabbing the affected parts with a piece of wadding soaked in lukewarm water.

CARE OF THE HATCHLINGS

Once the hatchlings are free-moving and have completely left the the eggshell, they should be taken from the incubator and placed in a "nursery" accommodation. Small glass or plastic aquarium tanks with ventilated lids are ideal and may be kept in a larger, heated terrarium or

underside.

With optimum conditions and a satisfactory diet, hatchling Green Iguanas will should start to feed within seven days (prior to this they will still be living on the contents of the yolk sac). An ideal diet for hatchling Green Iguanas is a mixture of green foods (lettuce, spinach, dandelion leaves and flowers, alfalfa, and clover) chopped into small pieces. This mixture can be sprinkled with small amounts of finely grated carrot, bone-meal, finely chopped

K. H. SWITAK

The best moment for a breeder of Green Iguanas is when a healthy hatchling crawls its way out of its egg.

dog food, or lean mince, and with a vitamin/mineral supplement added in at least three times per week. Additionally, the babies should each be given a daily helping of one or two mealworms, crickets, or other collected insects.

Should certain kinds of food be ignored, keep trying others until you arrive at a satisfactory feeding regime. Once a youngster starts taking one kind of food it will not be long before it is prepared to try others. Variety is the key to good health, especially in the vegetative part of the diet. Do not allow your Green Iguanas to eat only meats or insects or they may grow too fast, become obese, and then be useless for breeding. Some may also die prematurely. It is a good idea to weigh your specimens regularly and monitor their growth progress, furthermore keeping full records of all relative progress both for your own use and that of others in the future. As the reptiles grow, their rations of animal-based foods should be decreased and that of plant foods increased.

Above: Getting neonatal Green Iguanas to eat sometimes can be difficult. Often the mistake is on the keeper's part in regard to what foods are being offered. Photo by Isabelle Francais.

Over-feeding is also a bad habit many young keepers get into. Allowing a Green Iguana to become obese is not only irresponsible, but it endangers the animal's health. Artwork by John R. Quinn.

Right: Most newborn Green Iguanas are fairly willing feeders, so a keeper should do their best to quickly develop a diet for them that is as varied as possible.

W. P. MARA

In time, you may find your Green Iguanas eating just about anything! But be careful, however, that what you're giving them isn't too fatty. Macaroni, for example, is probably not a great Green Iguana food.

You should not be able to see the rib cage on a healthy, well-fed Green Iguana.

ISABELLE FRANCAIS

A VETERINARY PERSPECTIVE

Green Iguanas are fairly resistant to diseases and most cases of ill-health among captive stock may usually be blamed on some inadequacy in their care (although specimens often are already emaciated from the stresses and strains of importation). In recent research, good progress has been made into the diagnosis and treatment of reptile diseases and many hitherto "hopeless" cases can now be successfully treated. Increasing numbers of veterinarians are now concerning themselves with the treatment of exotic pets, including Green Iguanas, and veterinary colleges are even including such data in their curricula. If your local veterinarian is not sure about a particular case, he should be able to communicate with someone who could be. Green Iguana keepers should not try other than the simplest of home treatments on their pets but instead use the services of a veterinarian whenever possible.

SOME OF THE MORE USUAL CONDITIONS THAT MAY OCCUR ARE AS FOLLOWS:

Wounds and Injuries: These may be caused by escape attempts (especially with regard to rubbing the snout raw along the terrarium glass or mesh—this is common in newly captured wild specimens), lamp burns, fighting, etc., and are susceptible to infection. All open wounds should be treated immediately. Shallow wounds will usually heal automatically if swabbed daily with a mild antiseptic such as povidone-iodine. Deeper or badly infected wounds should be treated by a veterinarian in case surgery is required. Bone fractures, particularly in the limbs, may require some form of splinting in order to prevent malformation of the bone during healing. Again, your veterinarian should be consulted.

Nutritional Problems: These usually occur as a result of a lack of certain minerals or vitamins in the diet and are likely to affect Green Iguanas fed on a monotonous diet of, say, mealworms or lettuce. It is essential for Green Iguanas to

Above: One way to avoid health problems with Green Iguanas is to always make sure they get enough food, and the right food. Photo by Isabelle Francais.

Opposite: A healthy Green Iguana.

Although the crests on the back of this Green Iguana are slightly deteriorated, for the most part, the specimen shown is in fairly good shape.

All keepers should inspect their Green Iguanas at least once a month for signs of disease. Photo by Isabelle Francais.

have access to a large variety of food items plus regular vitamin/mineral supplements and an opportunity to bask in sunlight or full-spectrum light. The incidence of disease will thus be minimized dramatically dramatically.

Ectoparasites: The most usual external parasites associated with Green Iguanas are several species of ticks and mites. Ticks are often found attached to newly captured specimens and may range up to 0.25 in/6 mm in length. They fasten themselves with their piercing mouthparts to the lizard's skin, usually in a secluded spot between the scales (especially near the vent) or where the limbs join the body. Never attempt to pull a tick directly out because its head may be left embedded in the skin, causing infection later on. The tick's body should first be dabbed with a little alcohol (surgical spirit, meths, or even a drop of vodka) to relax the mouthparts. The tick can then be

gently twisted out with thumb and forefinger or with forceps.

Mites are much smaller than ticks and often multiply to large numbers before they are even noticed. A large mite infestation can cause dysecdysis, stress, loss of appetite, anemia, and eventual death. Mites are also capable of transmitting blood diseases from one reptile to another. The reptile mite is smaller than a pinhead, has a round body, and is grayish in color (though it will be red if it has recently sucked blood). Mites may be seen at night or when you switch the lights on early in the morning. Also, their tiny, silvery, powdery droppings may be seen on their host's skin. Mites are most often introduced to the terrarium with new stock, which is why all new specimens should be quarantined for at least two weeks before being housed with any of your existing pets.

Fortunately, mites can controlled quite easily by using a proprietary plastic insecticidal strip (of the type used to control houseflies). A small piece of such a strip placed in a perforated container and suspended in a terrarium will kill the mites in two to three days, after which time the strip is then removed. Since the strip does not kill mite eggs, the operation should be repeated ten days later to kill off any newly hatched mites. Two or three treatments will usually destroy all mites involved. It would be advisable also to spray the general areas around the terrarium with a surface spray insecticide, but do not use such a spray inside the terrarium itself because it could harm the animals themselves.

Endoparasites: The internal parasites with which we are mainly concerned are various species of worm that live in the alimentary canal and feed on a Green Iguana's partly digested food. In healthy Green Iguanas, worm numbers self-regulate and do not normally create major problems. In stressed or sick reptiles, however, the worms will proliferate or grow larger, taking more of the lizard's food. The toxic waste materials of large numbers of worms may be an additional problem. Worms are therefore undesirable in captive Green Iguanas because they can cause complications, anemia, and even death. By sending regular fecal samples to a veterinary laboratory you will have any worm infestations diagnosed. Various proprietary vermicides are available and your vet will be able to advise you of those specially suited for Green Iguanas. Some of these may be given with food but in severe cases you may have to get your vet to administer the medicine via stomach tube.

Bacterial Diseases: While there are many bacteria that are harmless (and even beneficial to normal body

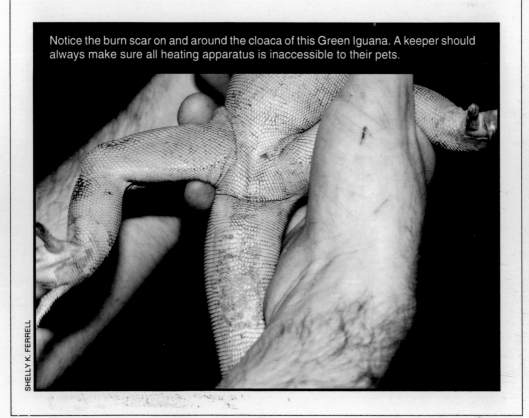

Notice the burn scar on and around the cloaca of this Green Iguana. A keeper should always make sure all heating apparatus is inaccessible to their pets.

SHELLY K. FERRELL

functions), other forms are pathogenic. Green Iguanas kept in unhygienic conditions are especially susceptible, so the importance of scrupulous cleanliness cannot be over-emphasized. Most bacterial infections respond well to antibiotic or other treatment if caught in the early stages of infection. Consult your veterinarian.

Salmonellosis: Salmonella poisoning is known to have been transmitted from reptiles to man (especially from freshwater turtles, although many *Salmonella* species have also been isolated from the feces of various lizards so the possibility of it occurring in Green Iguanas cannot be ruled out). It is therefore important to thoroughly wash the hands after each cleaning or handling session. Salmonellosis manifests itself in unhealthy, watery, green-colored, foul-odored feces. Antibiotic treatment will be carried out by your veterinarian.

Protozoa: These microscopic amoeba-like organisms cause infections of the gut. *Entamoeba invadans* is a fairly common protozoan infection which, untreated, will rapidly reach epidemic proportions in captive Green Iguanas. Symptoms include watery, slimy feces and general debility. Appropriate antibiotic treatment will be prescribed by your veterinarian.

Respiratory Infections: These may occasionally manifest themselves in stressed specimens. The patient will have difficulty breathing, the nostrils will be blocked, and there will be a nasal

Although visually unattractive, the molting of a Green Iguana's skin is a perfectly normal process (provided, of course, it all comes off).

JOHN DOMMERS

PHOTO BY W. P. MARA.

The head is a good place to check for early signs of ill health. Look at the eyes, are they watery? How about the mouth, does it close all the way? Are the gums swollen? And the nostrils, do they have any mucus running out of them?

discharge. Often the symptoms can be alleviated by moving the patient to warmer, drier, well-ventilated quarters. In severe cases, your veterinarian will recommend the appropriate treatment.

Skin Problems: There is a whole host of infections of the body surface which can be caused by fungi, bacteria, and viruses. Abscesses, which appear as lumps below the skin, are usually caused by infection building up in the flesh after the skin has been accidentally damaged. Skin infections should be referred to a veterinarian, who will give antimycotic, antiseptic, or antibiotic treatment. Deep infections and severe abscesses may be surgically opened, swabbed out, and then sutured, followed by a course of the appropriate medicines to prevent reinfection. Dysecdysis, the inability to shed properly (often as a result of a mite infestation or stress brought about by various other factors), may cause skin problems in Green Iguanas. Mite infestations should be cleared immediately and aid should be given to lizards experiencing difficulty sloughing. Healthy Green Iguanas will slough (molt) their skins, problem-free, several times per year; it is a natural phenomenon related to growth. The skin is normally shed in patches and the whole process should take no more than a few days. Disease organisms can grow behind persistent patches of old skin that do not come off readily. The skin can often be loosened and peeled off by placing the reptile in a bath of very shallow, warm water for about one or two hours.

TIDBITS STUDIO

Shown is the proper way to hold a Green Iguana. Improper handling is not only dangerous to the keeper, but to the animal as well.

TIDBITS STUDIO

The problem with using wooden cage decor is that once an item gets defecated on, it is very difficult to get completely clean again.

SUGGESTED READING

PS-311, 96 pgs, 60+ photos

SK-015, 64 pgs. 40+ photos

PS-316, 128 pgs, 100+ photos

KW-196, 128 pgs, 100+ photos

PS-769, 192 pgs, 120+ photos

TU-025, 64 pgs, 60+ photos

SK-032, 64 pgs, 40+ photso

YF-111, 32 pgs

TS-145, 288 pgs, 250+ photos

PS-207, 230 pgs, 100+ photos

H-935, 576 pgs, 260+ photos

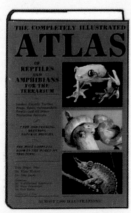

H-1102, 830 pgs, 1800+ Illus and photos

TS-165, VOL I, 655 pgs, 1850+ photos

TS-165, VOL II